YOU HAVE SOMETHING TO SAY

Use Your Voice.

YOU HAVE SOMETHING TO SAY... USE YOUR VOICE

© Copyright 2024.

All rights reserved. No part of this publication may be reproduced, distributed, or transmitted in any form or by any means, including photocopying, recording, or other electronic or mechanical methods, without the prior written permission of the publisher, except in the case of brief quotations embodied in critical reviews and certain other noncommercial uses permitted by copyright law. This book incorporates additional references from individuals who have authored one or two works to further articulate the concepts presented within. It is important to note that this is not intended to infringe upon the rights of any individual or to appropriate their ideas. We acknowledge and respect the contributions of all authors and creators.

First Printing edition 2024.

FOREWORD

This book is written for those who have allowed fear to silence their voice. Fear of rejection. Fear of failure. Fear of what others might say or think. Fear of success. Fear for physical safety. Fear of financial insecurity. Fear of the unknown. Fear of not being worthy. Fear of not being good enough. The list goes on and on. Which one applies to you? They all apply to me, and in this book, I will share my story and how the tools I've acquired throughout my life have helped me persevere and move forward despite these fears.

I was inspired to write this book after my husband passed 14 months ago (June 2023). His transition refocused my journey toward fulfilling my purpose and using my voice in this life. Whatever your fears, this book will give you the courage to confront them so you can use your voice because... "You have something to say, and it's powerful!"

"If there is one thing I've learned in life, it's the power of using your voice."

Michelle Obama

YOU HAVE SOMETHING TO SAY... USE YOUR VOICE

DEDICATION

This book is dedicated to my late husband,

Mark Duane Dixon

June 9, 1957 – June 15, 2023

TABLE OF CONTENTS

FOREWORD 2

DEDICATION 3

CHAPTER ONE: STATE OF MINDSET 6

CHAPTER TWO: FEAR 18

    WHAT IS FEAR? 18

    FEAR OF REJECTION 19

    FEAR OF FAILURE 20

    FEAR OF JUDGMENT 20

    FEAR OF THE UNKNOWN 21

CHAPTER THREE: VISION 29

CHAPTER FOUR: OPPORTUNITY 44

CHAPTER FIVE: INSPIRATION 62

CHAPTER SIX: COMMITMENT 78

CHAPTER SEVEN: ELEVATION 93

    ELEVATION – AMPLIFYING YOUR VOICE FOR GREATER IMPACT 93

THE FINAL CHAPTER 109

    THE POWER OF YOUR VOICE – A JOURNEY OF TRANSFORMATION 109

MINDSET: THE FOUNDATION FOR USING YOUR VOICE..109

FEAR: CONFRONTING THE SILENT ENEMY .. 110

VISION: SEEING BEYOND THE PRESENT........ 111

OPPORTUNITY: SAYING YES TO THE MOMENT 113

INSPIRATION: THE FUEL FOR YOUR VOICE ..114

COMMITMENT: THE SILENT FORCE BEHIND YOUR VOICE 115

ELEVATION: RISING TO NEW HEIGHTS WITH YOUR VOICE 115

YOUR VOICE MATTERS 116

CHAPTER ONE: STATE OF MINDSET

Romans 12:2 - "Do not conform to the pattern of this world but be transformed by the renewing of your mind. Then you will be able to test and approve what God's will is—his good, pleasing, and perfect will."

It all starts with my mindset. What we say and believe about ourselves sets the foundation for what we do.

I write this as much for myself as for anyone facing similar struggles. I have experienced all the fears mentioned above and more. These fears have kept me from fully stepping into my purpose because *I believed I was too different and not worthy of the same treatment as those around me*. Our mindset is deeply rooted in our beliefs about ourselves and the values that shape our reality, influencing our actions as we move through life.

From a young age, my life was shaped by contrasts and challenges. Growing up in a predominantly white, affluent community during the civil rights movement,

I faced daily struggles that went far beyond the typical experiences of childhood. My parents were civil rights activists, with my father serving as a minister and a prominent figure in the local and state chapters of the **National Association for the Advancement of Colored People (NAACP).** He frequently participated in events and spoke passionately about equality and justice. Day or night, he would often receive calls from Black individuals seeking representation as they faced legal challenges. At home, I was taught the importance of courage and resilience. Yet outside, the world seemed determined to stifle my spirit.

I was often bullied and teased by peers—both boys and girls—who mocked my differences with cruel laughter, harsh words, and inappropriate touches. This relentless bullying instilled a deep-seated fear, silencing me when I most wanted to speak out. The assassination of Martin Luther King Jr., a figure I equated with my father due to their shared passion for justice, only deepened my fears. I constantly worried that my father might meet the same fate, a fear that consumed my thoughts and further stifled my voice.

I witnessed how people of color were treated, not only in my local community but across the nation. I participated with my parents in non-violent marches and also witnessed protests that turned violent, where people who looked like me were treated as less than human. I became my father's protector, accompanying him to community, state, and church events. Although he tried to reassure me that nothing would happen to him, I still needed to stay by his side.

To soothe my fears, I turned to food for comfort. Over the years, this emotional eating led to significant weight gain, making me physically more extensive than most of my peers. Ironically, this change put an end to much of the bullying. No longer an easy target due to my size, I found peace in my newfound physical strength. While I still didn't use my voice, I learned that my hands could command respect whenever I felt threatened or disrespected.

It wasn't until high school that the bullying honestly stopped. By then, I had grown not only in size but also in understanding. The lessons learned at home, the legacy of the movement, and my parents' unyielding dedication to the cause had gradually infused me with a quiet strength. High school brought new environments and more accepting peers, allowing my true self to begin to emerge.

I took a Principles of Business class, which allowed me to join the **Distributive Education Clubs of America (DECA).** The course curriculum taught business principles, which students could immediately apply by running the school store and competing at the state level with students from other schools. By the time I was a junior, I had been selected as one of the Student Officers at the state level.

Our responsibilities required us to compete and organize the state convention where all schools competed. We attended monthly meetings as officers to learn public speaking, event planning and execution, and business etiquette and expand our knowledge about the DECA organization while working together as a team.

The positivity and validation were most impactful, as I found my voice due to that incredible experience... But did I?

The power of the mind is immense, and I can use it to achieve anything I desire. However, distractions are constant, making it crucial to stay focused to keep moving forward. Staying focused means that what I concentrate on will shape the quality of my life. If I focus on problems, they will grow, but if I focus on the good things, they will multiply. My life transformation begins when I decide, focus, and take action.

A positive mindset is essential for success but it hinges on your belief that you are Worthy...Full Stop!

I could end the book right here, as this truly is the key. But I won't because, believe it or not, I didn't fully grasp or articulate this understanding until recently. Yes, a woman of God in her 60s—with life, educational, and professional experience—who understood this intellectually but didn't believe it about herself. Maybe this sounds familiar; perhaps it could be you.

I fully embraced this in the past year while going through the grieving process after the passing of my husband. As a **"giver"** by nature, I felt free to give to myself for the first time in a long while. This year has been one of self-rediscovery and, most importantly, a reconnection with God. I attended a virtual webinar hosted by **Jamie Kern Lima, author of *Worthy*—** a book I highly recommend. I won't go into all the details (you should read the book), but it was the catalyst that illuminated an essential realization for me. Understanding the distinction between self-confidence (driven by external factors) and self-worth (driven by internal factors) and recognizing that both need to be nurtured was transformative. The concept that **"we rise to the level of our self-worth"** was compelling! (Again, get the book!)

While growing up as a Preacher's kid (PK), I practiced religion as required. Although this laid my spiritual foundation, it wasn't until I reached college that I actively sought a church connection and developed a personal relationship with God.

As I share the strategies that have helped me overcome my fears of using my voice, I do so with complete acceptance, belief, and the firm understanding that I am worthy—because God **says I am!**

Lessons Learned

- **I've learned to believe that I am worthy!**
- I've learned to use my mind positively, transforming abstract thoughts into reality. The mind is powerful and can manifest desires, so I focus on my goals and take inspired action.
- I get clear about what I want by asking myself the following questions: *What are my goals? What do I want to achieve?* Once I understand my goals, it becomes easier to stay focused on them.
- I've learned to visualize my achievements. I see myself reaching my goals and living my desired life, imagining myself taking inspired action every day.
- I've learned to believe in myself and my ability to achieve my goals. I understand that doubts can stifle my progress, so I consciously believe in my potential and strive to become the best version of myself.
- I've discovered the redemptive power of making firm decisions. By making a steadfast decision to change, I can transform my life.

- I've learned to take action. By taking inspired steps toward my goals, I see results, and my life changes.

Staying focused:

- I learned to simplify. One of my first steps is stripping my goals down to the essentials. Having multiple life goals is great, but focusing on too many at a time can be overwhelming.
- I have learned to analyze my goal list. What is most important right now? I prioritize my goals and focus on those that will create lasting change in my life.
- I now list all my objectives and choose the most essential ones.
- I focus on three vital tasks each day. I don't create massive to-do lists; I zoom in on the essentials and prioritize.
- When I take action and make progress toward my goals, it helps keep me motivated.
- Progress is essential for maintaining motivation, whether taking small steps or making significant strides.

Take action and make progress:

- I avoid overthinking. It's easier said than done, but it's essential if I want to take action and move forward. When I start to overthink, I take a deep breath and begin. It doesn't need to be perfect—what matters is starting, and everything else will follow.
- I break my goals into small, manageable steps. Since significant goals can feel overwhelming, I divide them into more straightforward tasks, gradually working toward the more critical objectives.
- Starting small helps me build self-confidence and resilience.
- I focus on the process. Concentrating on the journey rather than the destination, I stay motivated, engaged, and driven.

The Blessings of a Positive Mindset

- I take more risks. With a positive outlook, I see possibilities instead of obstacles. I'm more willing to take risks because I trust my ability to overcome challenges.

- I'm more resilient. A positive mindset helps me persevere. I understand that setbacks are temporary, and I am confident I will eventually reach my goals.
- I attract better opportunities. Maintaining a positive mindset naturally attracts positive people and new opportunities into my life.
- When I stay positive, I focus on my goals. I don't dwell on past failures or allow negative thoughts to hold me back. Instead, I view each challenge as an opportunity for learning and growth.

Using Your Voice....

What we say and believe about ourselves lays the foundation for everything we do. Growing up in a predominantly white community during the civil rights movement, with activist parents, put me in a unique and challenging position. My mindset made me feel ***"too different" and "not worthy."*** Romans 12:2 reminds us that transformation begins with the renewing of our minds.

Reflection Questions:

- What limiting beliefs about yourself are you holding onto?
- How has your mindset affected your ability to use your voice?
- What steps can you take today to start renewing your mind?

Exercise: Mindset Transformation

Step 1: Identify Limiting Beliefs

Write down three limiting beliefs you hold about yourself that stop you from using your voice.

Step 2: Challenge Your Beliefs

Next to each limiting belief, write a positive affirmation or truth that counters it.

Step 3: Create a Mindset Renewal Plan

Write down three practical actions you can take this week to challenge and renew your mindset. These actions can include daily affirmations, prayer, meditation, or any activity that helps shift your mindset positively.

CHAPTER TWO: FEAR

2 Timothy 1:7 - "For God has not given us a spirit of fear, but of power and of love and of a sound mind."

Fear is a powerful force that affects each of us in different ways. It can keep us silent when we should speak, paralyze us when action is necessary, and even distort our self-perception to the point where we begin to doubt our worth. When we use our voice, fear often becomes the silent stalker lurking in the background, ready to strike the moment we consider expressing ourselves. However, while fear is real, it is also conquerable—with practice and prayer.

WHAT IS FEAR?

At its core, fear is a natural response designed to protect us from danger. It triggers the body's fight-or-flight response, releasing hormones like adrenaline and cortisol that prepare us to face or flee from a perceived threat. However, many of our fears are not rooted in physical danger but in psychological and emotional threats of rejection, failure, judgment, and the unknown. These fears can become overwhelming, causing us to silence our voices when they are most needed.

2 Timothy 1:7 – "For God has not given us a spirit of fear, but of power, and of love, and of a sound mind."

This scripture is crucial because it reminds us that God did not intend for us to fear. The spirit He gives us is one of power and soundness of mind, not of anxiety or paralysis. When I reflect on what causes me to fear, rejection, failure, judgment, and the unknown are the most common.

FEAR OF REJECTION

I fear that if I speak up—whether it's sharing an opinion, asking for something I need, or standing up for myself—I might be rejected by those around me. This fear is deeply rooted in the human need for acceptance and belonging.

Proverbs 29:25 – "The fear of man brings a snare, but whoever trusts in the Lord shall be safe."

The fear of rejection often stems from placing too much value on others' opinions, creating a trap. This proverb reminds us that trusting in God frees us from this snare, emphasizing that our value comes from Him, not from the approval of others.

FEAR OF FAILURE

When I try something that fails, I confirm my worst nightmare: that I am not good enough or capable. This fear of failure can be so debilitating that it prevents me from ever trying, stifling my potential before I even begin.

Isaiah 41:10 – "So do not fear, for I am with you; do not be dismayed, for I am your God. I will strengthen you and help you; I will uphold you with my righteous right hand."

God assures us that even in our weakest moments, He is there to uphold and strengthen us. Failure is not the end; instead, it is an opportunity to lean into His strength and keep moving forward.

FEAR OF JUDGMENT

I often worry about what others think or say if I speak up. Will they ridicule me? Will they judge me harshly?

This fear of judgment can be extreme in social situations where everyone's eyes are on me.

Romans 8:31 – "What, then, shall we say in response to these things? If God is for us, who can be against us?"

When we allow the fear of judgment to control our lives, we forget that the ultimate judgment comes from God. His opinion is what truly matters. No one else's judgment holds any real power if God is for us.

FEAR OF THE UNKNOWN

Sometimes, fear stems from not knowing what will happen when I speak up. Will there be a conflict? Will I lose something? The unknown can feel like an insurmountable barrier, keeping me trapped in a state of inaction.

Psalm 56:3 – "When I am afraid, I put my trust in you."

Though the unknown may feel frightening, God calls us to trust Him. When we place our faith in Him, we can move forward, even when the path is unclear.

Lessons Learned

Habits Can Remove Fears

- My fears become ingrained very quickly because avoiding what causes fear only makes it stronger. For example, if I ask my boss for a raise, I immediately feel anxious. If I avoid asking for that raise, I feel instant relief. My brain just learned a quick lesson: feel afraid, prevent the behavior, and feel better.
- Avoidance is like a drug. It provides a quick way to relieve myself of fear. The best way to ensure I avoid a behavior is to generate physical sensations of fear, creating a challenging cycle to break.
- Creating new habits is one way I can gradually eliminate my fears. I can form habits that promote new responses to fear in general and habits tailored to address specific worries.
- Developing the Habit of Courage: Those who possess courage aren't without fear. If I weren't afraid, I wouldn't need courage in the first place! Courage is acting in the presence of fear; it is

ultimately a habit that must be cultivated daily until it becomes automatic.

I try these strategies to develop my courage:

- Confront my fear.
- I try holding my ground for a change.
- I avoid distracting myself or avoiding the situation.
- I sit with those uncomfortable feelings and give them my full attention. I notice how those feelings dissipate within a few minutes.
- Expect success. Things work out for the best in the end. When I expect a positive outcome, fear is difficult to maintain.
- Stay with reality. How many failures have I had that created long-term challenges for me? Very few. It's easy to develop disastrous scenarios in my mind, but that's the only place they exist. Realistically, I have little risk in most situations. The most fearful situations have the most significant rewards.
- Evaluate the risk/reward ratio for my situation. I try to make a logical decision and ignore what my body tells me. My body is lying to me.

- Challenge myself. Fears go away when I keep pushing forward. When fear fails to stop me from acting, my brain will realize it's a strategy that no longer works. It's worth the effort to learn to act more courageously and consistently. This habit carries over to every part of my life. When fear is no longer steering my decisions, life becomes much more accessible. I remember that fear is just a physical sensation. It doesn't have to direct my actions.
- I embrace the discomfort. Be excited. When I'm experiencing discomfort, it means I'm doing something that can make a real difference in my life. When I spend an entire day feeling a little pain, I can bet that good things are happening.
- Relax. I relax my shoulders and all the other muscles in my body. That tenseness that occurs when I'm afraid sets off a chain reaction that creates even more discomfort. Simply relaxing my muscles can relieve a lot of pain.
- Breathe. Shallow, uneven breathing creates physiological changes that generate more physical discomfort. My breathing is one thing I

can control. I take deeper, slower breaths and watch what happens.

- Be curious. Instead of putting myself into a state of mental distress when the uncomfortable feelings begin, I ask myself a few questions: "That's an interesting feeling. I wonder why I'm feeling this way. " What is the worst that can happen? How could I handle that?" "How great will I feel if I don't give up this time?" By directing my attention, I can stop the fear from growing out of control.
- Stay present. Fear grows when I allow my thoughts to drift to unpleasant places. I keep my mind focused on the present moment. I avoid imagining the worst.
- Discomfort can be my friend. It signals that I'm taking action that has the potential to improve my life. Rather than running from fear, I consider running toward it.

You will notice the word **VOICE** in the book title, is an Acronym for Vision, Opportunity, Inspiration, Commitment, and Elevation. Each is a separate chapter and is offered as a component of the elements needed to use our voice. I start each chapter with a relevant scripture related to the title as I am God Inspired and then share my personal story related to that chapter. You will also notice that Biblical scriptures are sprinkled throughout as they serve as my foundation in life. I continue to end each chapter with Lessons Learned and then offer the reader the opportunity to Use Their Voice... with questions to reflect on and exercises to apply.

Using *Your* Voice...

Fear of rejection, judgment, and failure has often kept me from using my voice. While fear is a natural response, it doesn't come from God. To conquer fear, we must embrace power, love, and sound thinking.

Reflection Questions:

What fears have held you back from speaking up?

How can you confront those fears and step into your power?

What will it look like for you to use your voice despite fear?

Exercise: Stepping Beyond Fear

Step 1: Name Your Fears

Write down three fears that have kept you from speaking up.

Step 2: Reframe Your Fears

Next to each fear, write a sentence that reframes it in a way that empowers you. For example, *"I fear rejection" becomes "Rejection is an opportunity to grow and refine my message."*

Step 3: Create a Fear Action Plan

For each fear, write one action step you can take to confront it. For example, if you fear public speaking, commit to sharing your thoughts in a small group or family setting as a first step.

CHAPTER THREE: VISION

Proverbs 29:18 says, "Where there is no vision, the people perish: but he that keepeth the law, happy is he."

Vision – The Guiding Light to Using Your Voice

My mother, as the first female role model in my life, had no problem using her voice. She could use it to both lift you and tear you down. She set high expectations for those she loved, and if you failed to meet them, she would make it clear in no uncertain terms. Her words could crush your spirit and challenge your sense of self-worth. I witnessed many of her interactions with my father, where her words would challenge his identity as a man and the many roles he filled. Often, I was his confidant, listening as he shared the devastation her words caused and the emotional toll it took on him.

Watching the effects of my mother using her voice intimidated me and silenced me. I constantly tried to meet her expectations, often feeling like I failed as she guided my path. I always felt that everything I did was good enough for her. You may wonder, what does this have to do with vision?

My mother's vision for me was to graduate high school, attend college, earn a degree, get married, and have children by age 23. Oh, and I was supposed to meet the man I would marry in college. Notice that I said *my mother's vision for me*, not *mine*. From a very young age, I adopted her vision, trying to meet her expectations and often falling short, which deepened my unworthiness. This feeling peaked when I graduated college, and the only prospect for a husband was someone I loved but could never have.

My focus shifted to obtaining my first job after college. I returned home to live with my parents, feeling fear, anger, and low self-worth. I was angry at my mother because she often reminded me that I hadn't met the expectations she had for me. Fortunately, after six months, I secured a job at American Express in New York. My sister worked there, and I planned to move in with her once I started working. Looking back, I was still trying to fulfill my mother's vision of finding a husband and starting a family. I dated different men, but none felt like someone I could see as my husband. Then, at a coworker's birthday party, I met a man whose mother and family were from the Virgin Islands, just like my mother. He was deeply knowledgeable about our Black culture and history, which instantly drew me to him.

His vast knowledge reminded me of my father; we shared many cultural interests. His family was Muslim, which was new and intriguing to me. By this time, I had moved out of my sister's place and was living on my own. We had been dating for several months before I met his family, and now it was time for him to meet mine. I had moved back in with my parents by then. My mother was already hesitant about our relationship because he was from the city, while I was from the suburbs. She had labeled him a "city slicker," deeming him unsuitable for her daughter, even before meeting him.

Once again, I failed to meet her expectations. While she was polite, she was neither warm nor welcoming. On the other hand, my father was gracious and kind, as he always was with everyone. Not long after, I became pregnant with our son. He and I shared the news with my parents together.

By now, you can probably imagine my mother's response. This was, in her eyes, the ultimate disappointment. She could not believe I had let something like this happen, especially after all she had sacrificed and invested in me. Her words to him reminded me of the many times she spoke to my father in a demeaning way. We ended the conversation by informing them that we would be getting married, which we did three months later. Once again, I used my actions rather than my voice to convey my message.

Vision is more than just a plan or a goal; it is the guiding light that illuminates the path ahead, giving purpose to our words, actions, and existence. When it comes to using your voice, vision is crucial. Without it, we can quickly become lost in fear, doubt, and confusion. This is especially true when you are living someone else's vision—the guiding light is not your own, causing you to react to life moment by moment.

Vision brings clarity, helping you find your voice and use it with intention, confidence, and impact.

At its core, vision is the ability to see beyond your current circumstances. It involves imagining a future where your voice makes a meaningful difference—whether in your community, family, or global stage. Vision connects the dots between where you are now and where you want to be. It also inspires you to speak with purpose, understanding that your words are part of a larger narrative.

Proverbs 29:18 – "Where there is no vision, the people perish: but he that keepeth the law, happy is he."

This verse from Proverbs underscores the vital importance of vision. Without it, there is chaos, stagnation, and a lack of direction. Vision helps us prioritize what matters and guides our actions, ensuring we remain purposeful. In using your voice, a clear vision gives you the confidence to speak up because you recognize how your words fit into the bigger picture of your life and the world around you.

With a clear vision, you understand who you are, what you stand for, and where you want to go. This clarity allows you to communicate with purpose and confidence. Your voice becomes a tool for expressing your vision, enabling you to share your dreams, goals, and beliefs with others in an authentic and impactful way.

Habakkuk 2:2 – "Then the Lord replied: 'Write down the revelation and make it plain on tablets so that a herald may run with it."

This scripture reminds me that vision must be clear and tangible. By writing down your vision, you not only make it understandable for others, but you also create a guide for yourself. When your vision is clear, your voice will naturally follow, becoming a powerful instrument for spreading your message and fulfilling your purpose.

Speaking up can be challenging for me, especially when faced with adversity or opposition. However, developing a solid vision has helped me overcome fear and doubt. When you're passionate about your vision, it compels you to speak out, even when it's uncomfortable. Your vision becomes more important than the fear of rejection or judgment.

Isaiah 41:10 – "So do not fear, for I am with you; do not be dismayed, for I am your God. I

will strengthen you and help you; I will uphold you with my righteous right hand."

God promises to be with me when I step out in faith. When I speak from a place of vision, I trust that He will give me the strength and courage to use my voice for His purpose.

Without a clear vision, our words can become scattered and aimless. However, when we have direction, our voice becomes focused and intentional. Vision acts as a compass, guiding our conversations, decisions, and actions. It helps align our voice with our values and goals, ensuring that we communicate in ways that move us closer to our vision.

James 1:5 – "If any of you lacks wisdom, let him ask of God, who gives to all liberally and without reproach, and it will be given to him."

When seeking direction, we are encouraged to ask God for wisdom. This wisdom shapes our vision and guides us in how we communicate and use our voice effectively.

Discovering your vision can be challenging. However, by following a few practical steps and relying on biblical principles, you can clarify your vision and begin using your voice with greater purpose and intention.

Your vision should be rooted in what matters most to you. Take time to reflect on your core values and passions. What excites you? What issues, causes, or topics do you care about deeply? By identifying these essential elements, you can form a vision that aligns with who you are and what you stand for.

Matthew 6:21: "For where your treasure is, there your heart will be also."

This verse reminds us that our vision should reflect what we truly treasure. When we align our voice with what is in our hearts, we speak from a place of authenticity and conviction.

Once you've reflected on your values and passions, the next step is to create a vision statement. This statement should be clear, concise, and inspirational. It should capture what you want to achieve and the impact you want to have through your voice.

Jeremiah 29:11 – "For I know the plans I have for you," declares the Lord, "plans to prosper you and not to harm you, plans to give you hope and a future."

God has a plan and purpose for each of us. Your vision statement reflects that plan, and aligning it with His will becomes a powerful tool for good.

A vision without action is merely a dream. To bring your vision to life, it's essential to break it down into specific, actionable goals. These goals will serve as a roadmap for using your voice to achieve your vision.

Proverbs 16:3 – "Commit to the Lord whatever you do, and He will establish your plans."

When we commit our goals to the Lord, He blesses our efforts and provides the strength and clarity we need to accomplish them.

Visualization is a powerful tool that can help you stay focused on your vision and motivated to use your voice. By imagining yourself successfully speaking up and making an impact, you train your mind to believe in the possibility of success.

Hebrews 11:1: "Now faith is confidence in what we hope for and assurance about what we do not see."

Visualization is an act of faith. When we visualize our success, we are exercising our belief in the vision God has given us, trusting that He will help us bring it to fruition.

Your daily actions should reflect your vision. If your vision is to inspire others through your words, ensure your actions align with that goal. This means speaking with integrity, being consistent in your messaging, and making choices that bring you closer to your vision.

Colossians 3:17: "And whatever you do, whether in word or deed, do it all in the name of the Lord Jesus, giving thanks to God the Father through him."

Our words and actions should reflect the vision God has placed in our hearts. When we align our actions with our vision, we honor God and significantly impact the world.

Vision is the foundation for discovering and using your voice. It provides clarity, direction, and inspiration, enabling you to speak with confidence and purpose. By reflecting on your values, creating a vision statement, setting actionable goals, and aligning your actions with your vision, you can overcome fear and doubt, using your voice to make a lasting impact.

Remember, your vision is a gift from God, and through His strength, you will accomplish the goals He has placed in your heart. Trust in His guidance, speak boldly, and let your vision lead you toward greatness.

Habakkuk 2:3 – "For the vision is yet for an appointed time; but at the end it shall speak, and not lie: though it tarry, wait for it; because it will surely come, it will not tarry."

Lessons Learned

Vision is the cornerstone of effective communication. It's the ability to see beyond my current reality and imagine the impact of my voice. This chapter delves into how I can develop a clear and compelling vision that guides my communication efforts and empowers me to overcome the fears that have held me back. By crafting a solid vision, I align my message with my purpose, making my voice heard and felt.

A well-defined vision serves as a beacon, guiding my message and actions. It's not just about knowing what I want to say but also understanding why it matters and who will benefit from it. Here's why a strong vision is crucial for me:

- **Clarity of Purpose:** A clear vision helps me articulate my message accurately, reducing ambiguity and enhancing impact.
- **Motivation and Focus:** It fuels my drive to overcome obstacles and stay committed, even when faced with fears or setbacks.
- **Alignment:** Ensures that my communication efforts align with my core values and goals, making my message more authentic and compelling.
- **Reflect on My Passions:** I ask myself what topics or issues ignite a fire within me. My vision should align with what I care deeply about.
- **Consider My Audience:** I think about who I am trying to reach. My vision should speak to their needs and aspirations.
- **Combine Vision Elements:** I draft a statement incorporating my passions and audience needs. I refine it until it's clear and motivating.
- **Authenticity:** I ensure my vision reflects who I truly am. Authenticity builds trust and credibility.

- **Consistency:** My vision should be consistently reflected in my messaging, whether through spoken words, written content, or online presence.
- **Adaptability:** I remain open to refining my vision as I grow and learn more.
- **Reframe Failure:** I view setbacks as opportunities for growth rather than indicators of inadequacy.
- **Visualize Success:** I regularly imagine the successful outcome of my efforts. This positive reinforcement helps diminish my fears.
- **Seek Support:** I surround myself with people who support my vision and encourage me.
- **Vision Board:** I visually represent my vision using images, words, and symbols that inspire me. I place it where I can see it daily.
- **Success Stories:** I read or listen to stories of others who have achieved similar goals. This reinforces my belief in my success.
- **Adapt and Adjust:** I am flexible and willing to adapt my vision as circumstances change.

- **Celebrate Progress:** I recognize and celebrate small victories to maintain motivation.

Using *Your* Voice...

Living under the weight of my mother's vision for me was challenging, but learning to seek out my vision and align it with God's purpose transformed my life. Vision provides clarity and direction for using your voice effectively.

Reflection Questions:

- What is your vision for how your voice can impact the world?
- How clear is your vision, and what steps can you take to refine it?
- How does your vision give you the strength to continue using your voice?

Exercise: Clarifying Your Vision

Step 1: Identify Your Passion

Write down what excites and motivates you. What do you care deeply about? List three passions that align with how you want to use your voice.

Step 2: Craft Your Vision Statement

Write a one- or two-sentence vision statement for how you want your voice to impact the world. This statement should be clear and align with your values.

Step 3: Set Visionary Goals

List three specific goals you can set for the next six months that will help you move closer to fulfilling your vision. These include joining a community group, starting a blog, or mentoring others.

CHAPTER FOUR: OPPORTUNITY

Colossians 4:5 - *"Be wise in the way you act toward outsiders; make the most of every opportunity."*

This past year has been a journey I never anticipated, filled with grief, healing, and opportunities I never thought I would encounter. After the transition of my husband, my internal world was shaken. But God knows what we can handle, and He always provides for us. He orchestrated my daughter's temporary relocation to Cleveland two months prior. Her presence has been a soft landing in the wake of his transition, filling the emptiness and silence in the house. In feeling the absence of his voice, I realized the lack of my own. I found myself in a space where I had to decide whether to continue in silence or step forward into a new chapter, where I would use my voice in ways I hadn't before.

At first, the idea of saying yes to anything felt overwhelming. I was trying to survive the loss and navigate the emptiness that came with it. But then something shifted within me. I realized that while my husband was no longer physically present, I was still here. I still had a purpose, and opportunities were unfolding that I could embrace or let pass by. I decided to say yes, to use my voice, to step into the unknown, and to embrace the opportunities that came my way—even if they scared me.

One of the first opportunities I embraced was joining a new church. After relocating to be with my husband, I went on a church tour for several years. Although he did not attend, I found it essential to go, as church has always been a significant part of my life. When the pandemic struck, I began attending online services. After the pandemic ended, I continued participating sporadically and eventually stopped altogether.

After my husband passed away, I felt disconnected from the community and the world around me. I needed a place to feel anchored and to connect with people who understood the weight of life's challenges. My daughter, sharing a similar desire, also began attending. While it was initially overwhelming, it became one of the best decisions I made. The music, the message, and the community spoke to me, offering much-needed support and encouragement.

Not long after that, the opportunity to become a certified reinvention strategist was presented to me—something that both excited and terrified me. Reinvention has been my life over the past year. Since my husband's transition, I have had to reinvent almost every aspect of my existence. My identity as a wife was no longer valid, and I needed to rediscover who I was as a woman standing on her own. Stepping into this new role meant that I would be sharing my journey and helping others navigate their transitions in life.

The first time I shared my story with the other members of this reinvention group, I felt that familiar wave of fear. Would my voice matter? Would anyone care about what I had to say? However, as I began speaking, I realized my story was a bridge for others. While our experiences differed, our desire to hone our skills was the same, and we supported each other in our applications. My voice became a catalyst for change, and in helping others, I found a more profound sense of purpose for myself.

My husband's transition forced me to confront my mortality and jolted me into organizing my estate affairs for when I die. While we discussed this topic, we didn't put anything in writing. Now that he was gone, I wanted to ensure my affairs wouldn't burden my children when my time came. I found a financial advisor and an attorney who helped me through this process. I realized it was also an opportunity to use my voice differently—one focused on legacy and preparation. In documenting my wishes, I essentially told my story—what mattered to me, what I valued, and how I wanted my life to be remembered.

Setting up my estate brought me peace, allowing me to speak more freely about life, death, and everything. It gave me the courage to talk openly with my loved ones about my plans and hopes for the future. In doing so, I encouraged them to think about their legacies and how they might use their voices while they still had the chance.

Another unexpected opportunity arose when I was invited to join a women's spiritual support group. At first, I wasn't sure if I wanted to be part of another group. I was already opening up in church, sharing my journey as a reinvention strategist, and managing my personal affairs. Did I really need another space to use my voice?

The answer was yes. This group became a safe space where I could let down my guard even further. The women in this group weren't just friends—they were sisters in Christ, each living her journey. We listened to each other's fears, doubts, and hopes while being inspired and growing in God's word and purpose for our lives. We were given biblical reading assignments and questions for reflection and application. At first, I was hesitant to share, as I found my story to be minor compared to others that were shared. However, I realized it didn't have to be major or minor; it was a safe space to be vulnerable, filled with a raw honesty that only comes when you feel supported.

Through this group, I learned the importance of having spaces where we can speak our truth without fear of judgment. It reminded me that our voice isn't just about what we say but about being present for others as they also find the courage to speak.

Writing this book was one of the most significant opportunities and surprises I accepted. My preference has always been to keep things to myself; writing was the last thing I enjoyed doing. Several women in the spiritual women's group had already written books, including the facilitator. One of the assignments in the group was to identify an area we needed to strengthen in our spiritual walk, and I recognized that journaling was my area for growth (God-inspired). We were tasked with creating an action plan detailing the steps to move forward and overcome this challenge. I developed the action plan and began implementing the steps documented in it.

As I applied these steps, God revealed what I should journal each morning just before waking up. I would remember His words and could journal them immediately upon awakening. In this process, He told me that I would write this book, which He named *You Have Something to Say... Use Your Voice*. Thus, this book was born.

It has been one of the most freeing experiences of my life. It has allowed me to reflect on my journey, process my grief, and see how far I've come. More importantly, it has allowed me to use my voice to help others. Through these pages, I hope to encourage anyone who feels their voice doesn't matter. I want to show them that they have something valuable to share no matter where they are in life.

Finally, I said yes to going to Hawaii—something that had felt like a dream I couldn't attain because my husband never liked traveling by plane or boat and didn't want to visit any tropical destinations. After he passed, I permitted myself to say yes. I had planned to take the trip with my daughter around my birthday. When the time came, the weather became an impediment, and I took it as a sign that it wasn't meant for me to go. Maybe it was my wish but not God's plan, so I held off on rebooking the trip for a couple of months. I finally rebooked it for Mother's Day. God's delays are not always His denials. That trip became more than just a vacation—it was a chance to disconnect from the everyday and reconnect with myself and him on another level, to reflect on all the opportunities I had said yes to, and to give myself the space to breathe.

Sitting on the beach in Hawaii, I realized that every opportunity I embraced over the past year was part of a more extensive journey. Each decision to use my voice was a step toward healing, growth, and purpose. I wasn't the same person I had been a year ago, and by saying yes to these opportunities, I discovered my voice in ways I never thought possible.

If there's one thing I've learned through all of this, it's that opportunities to use your voice are everywhere. You don't have to wait for the perfect moment or circumstances. Sometimes, the opportunity comes as a quiet nudge or an invitation that feels too big. But if I've learned anything, saying yes can change your life.

I encourage you to embrace the opportunities that come your way. Say yes, even when it feels scary or overwhelming. Trust that your voice matters, and by using it, you can make a difference for yourself and those around you. Your story is powerful, and the world needs to hear it. So, take that first step. Say yes. Use your voice and watch how your life—and the lives of others—begin to transform.

Opportunity is like a door suddenly opening, inviting you to walk through and take action. Throughout my life, I've learned that using your voice is often tied to recognizing and seizing the opportunities that arise. Sometimes, these opportunities are obvious—an invitation to speak or a chance to share your story—but they often come disguised as challenges or small moments that require courage.

Opportunity is connected to using your voice because it is the vessel through which your message reaches others. Recognizing and acting on opportunities is necessary for your voice to be heard. Through these moments, you can amplify your message, inspire others, and make a meaningful impact. Learning to see and seize opportunities to use my voice has been an ongoing process of growth and discovery.

Opportunities are everywhere, yet we often fail to recognize them because they don't come in the form we expect. Sometimes, we wait for an ample, obvious opportunity—a platform, a stage, or a grand invitation. However, more often than not, opportunities manifest as everyday conversations, quiet moments, or unexpected situations.

I recall many times when I hesitated to speak up, thinking it wasn't the "right" moment or that what I had to say wasn't important enough. Looking back, I realize those were missed opportunities. I've learned that every moment presents a chance to use my voice—whether in a simple conversation with a friend, standing up for what's right, or having the courage to speak out in difficult situations.

Ephesians 5:15-16 — "Be very careful, then, how you live—not as unwise but as wise, making the most of every opportunity, because the days are evil."

This scripture reminds me that opportunities are precious, and I must make the most of them. It calls for vigilance, wisdom, and readiness to speak up when the moment arises.

Recognizing an opportunity is one thing, but seizing it is another. Fear often holds us back from taking action. I've experienced this countless times—feeling the urge to speak up but too afraid of judgment, rejection, or failure. I've learned that opportunities don't always come twice, and hesitation might mean missing the chance to make an impact.

Seizing an opportunity requires boldness. It demands stepping outside your comfort zone and trusting that what you have to say is valuable. One of the most significant shifts in my life came when I stopped waiting for the perfect moment and started speaking up, even when it felt uncomfortable. I realized that I was permitting myself to use my voice by taking action.

One of my most significant revelations is that opportunities often come disguised as challenges. There have been times when I faced difficult situations, and my initial reaction was to shy away or stay silent. However, I've learned that challenges are often God's way of allowing us to grow and use our voice.

For instance, it would have been easier to remain silent when confronted with injustice or unfairness. Yet, I realized these challenges were opportunities to stand up for what I believe in and use my voice to make a difference. While it's not always easy, challenges provide us with a platform to speak the truth, offer solutions, and be a voice for change.

James 1:2-3 – "Consider it pure joy, my brothers and sisters, whenever you face trials of many kinds, because you know that the testing of your faith produces perseverance."

This scripture reminds me that challenges are often opportunities in disguise. When I face trials, I see them as chances to use my voice to strengthen my faith and influence those around me.

While it's important to recognize and seize the opportunities that come our way, I've learned that sometimes we need to create our own. Early in my journey, I waited for someone to permit me or invite me to use my voice. Eventually, I realized that I might never get the chance if I kept waiting.

Creating opportunities means being proactive. It's about taking initiative—starting a conversation, volunteering to speak, or finding ways to share your message with others. When I began creating my opportunities, doors started to open. I wasn't just waiting for a platform; I was building it.

One of the biggest obstacles to seizing opportunities is fear. I know this all too well because fear has often kept me from stepping into opportunities (and still does from time to time) that were right in front of me. The fear of failure, rejection, or criticism can be paralyzing. However, I've come to understand that fear is simply a barrier between me and the opportunity God has placed before me.

Lessons Learned

- I've learned courage isn't the absence of fear—it's taking action despite it. Whenever I push through the fear and speak up, I'm reminded that my voice is powerful and I have something worth saying. The more I practice seizing opportunities despite my fear, the easier it becomes to use my voice confidently.

- ***2 Timothy 1:7 – "For God has not given us a spirit of fear, but of power and of love and of a sound mind."***

- This verse has been a constant source of encouragement for me. It reminds me that fear is not from God. He has equipped me with power, love, and a sound mind—everything I need to seize the opportunities He places before me.

- Opportunities are not random; they are deeply connected to your purpose. Every chance I've had to use my voice was placed in my path for a reason. God doesn't waste anything; every moment—big or small—can be an opportunity to fulfill your purpose.

- I've found that opportunities flow more naturally when I align my voice with my purpose. The key is to stay open to the possibilities around me and recognize that every opportunity to speak is a step closer to fulfilling the mission God has placed on my heart.
- ***Jeremiah 29:11 – "For I know the plans I have for you, declares the Lord, plans to prosper you and not to harm you, plans to give you hope and a future."***
- This scripture reassures me that every opportunity is part of God's plan for my life. He has a purpose for my voice, and as I step into the opportunities He presents, I walk in alignment with His divine purpose.
- I've learned that opportunity favors the prepared. There have been times when a chance to use my voice came unexpectedly, and I wasn't ready. Whether it was a lack of confidence, preparation, or clarity, I missed the chance because I wasn't prepared.
- I've realized that I need to be prepared in advance to make the most of the opportunities that come my way. This means honing my skills,

staying clear on my message, and being ready to speak up. When preparation meets opportunity, powerful things happen.

- One of the most freeing things I've learned is that I don't have to create or control every opportunity that comes my way. God is the ultimate orchestrator of opportunities, and I've found that when I trust Him, He opens doors that I never could have imagined.

- There have been moments when I thought I missed an opportunity or felt discouraged because I wasn't seeing progress. But every time, God showed me that His timing is perfect. I find peace when I focus on being faithful to the opportunities He gives me rather than trying to force things to happen.

- ***Proverbs 3:5-6 – "Trust in the Lord with all your heart and lean not on your own understanding; in all your ways submit to him, and he will make your paths straight."***

- This verse reminds me that when I trust God with my opportunities, He will clear the path.

My job is to be ready, faithful, and willing to use my voice when the time comes.

- Opportunities surround us, but we must recognize, seize, and sometimes create them. Using your voice is not just about waiting for the perfect moment—it's about stepping into it.

Using *Your* Voice...

The loss of my husband gave me a new perspective on the opportunities in front of me. Each opportunity—from joining a new church to becoming a reinvention strategist—was a moment to say yes to using my voice. Opportunities are all around us, but they often come disguised as challenges or small moments of decision. By saying yes to these moments, I found that my voice could inspire, uplift, and create change. The more I embraced each opportunity, the more my voice grew.

Reflection Questions:

- What opportunities are in front of you right now to use your voice?
- What have you said no to because of fear or doubt?
- How can you start saying yes to more opportunities today?

Exercise: Seizing Opportunities

Step 1: Reflect on Missed Opportunities

Write down two or three opportunities you didn't take because of fear, doubt, or uncertainty.

Step 2: Identify Current Opportunities

List three current opportunities to use your voice (e.g., conversations, work presentations, community involvement).

Step 3: Take Action

For each opportunity, write one step you will take this week to say yes and use your voice. Be specific about the time and place where you will take this action.

CHAPTER FIVE: INSPIRATION

2 Timothy 3:16-17: "All Scripture is God-breathed and is useful for teaching, rebuking, correcting, and training in righteousness, so that the servant of God may be thoroughly equipped for every good work."

My father was my hero and my inspiration. He stood at 5 feet 3 inches, with dark, beautiful skin and hazel eyes. He was the kindest, most empathetic, and considerate person I have ever known. I feel so blessed to have had him as a father. He was incredibly compassionate, always using his voice to stand up for himself and others. He had a special tenderness in his heart for women raising children as single parents, likely because his mother passed away while giving birth to him.

His father, unable to care for him and his two siblings alone, placed them in an orphanage. He would visit them occasionally, and he remembered how they would watch him walk away from the orphanage gates after each visit, always after handing them each a banana and saying goodbye. One day, he explained that he had met a woman with children of her own and could no longer care for them. It was the last time he said goodbye. The siblings were eventually placed in different foster homes as they grew older. His sister, a few years older than him, stayed in contact with him throughout.

She would eventually tell him that the foster father was sexually abusing her, and she became impregnated by him. My father dropped out of high school at 16 to get a job on a chicken farm and find a small apartment to bring his sister and her daughter to live with him. The chicken farm was adjacent to an all-white wealthy community where generations of families lived in large homes, some with farms. During this time of segregation, black people were brought in as the help. Some were live-in help; some could have studios or one-bedroom apartments on one street upstairs above small businesses. They all attended the same church with a hall downstairs where they would assemble on their day off.

He met my mother after being previously married, having a daughter from that union, and eventually divorcing. My mother and he ultimately married. He was a devoted husband and father, always encouraging and supporting his family and others. They first bought a house in a community near where they met. Although the area was more integrated and closer to the church they attended, the school system was inadequate. Their goal was always to buy a home in the community where they first met, which they achieved once segregation ended. They became the second Black family to purchase a home there—my godparents were the first. Realtors would only show homes to Black families on one street.

My father realized this when the third Black family moved next to us. He approached the realtors and demanded that they show all available houses to Black families, not just those on our street. He would speak out when business owners still tried to segregate Black people in the community. While "Colored" signs came down, behaviors were slow to change. My father spoke up and held them accountable to the law in every instance. Everyone knew who he was and what he stood for, and he earned the respect of the entire community.

He eventually obtained a charter to start a National Association for the Advancement of Colored People (NAACP) branch in the community. This required a specific number of members. With only a few Black families in the area, they went door to door to recruit members and collect dues. The community was very supportive and quickly exceeded the membership requirement to secure the charter. They held meetings to discuss ways to support and integrate Black residents into the community. Over time, they expanded to include a youth charter. My father eventually became the President at the state level and an activist in the civil rights movement. We attended conferences and participated in marches for the cause.

He eventually returned to a supportive role as young activists rose to carry the torch. They honored my father by designating an annual award to someone who serves with great dedication. At the same time, our family was deeply involved in the church. My parents sang in the choir and served in various other roles. They were also socially active, frequently hosting parties and events. I remember when my dad felt "called" to become a minister. I was nine, and it was a significant moment in our lives. He shared the experience with my mother first, then with my brothers and me. He explained that he had awoken at night and felt led to kneel and pray.

As he did so, a light shone down on him from the ceiling, and he heard the voice of God telling him to become a minister and move forward in delivering God's word to His people.

He remembered becoming emotional as he heard this, feeling the weight of purpose and responsibility placed on his shoulders. He shared with us that, in this role, he would need to step back from certain social activities and expand his service in the community to align with his new assignment. Shortly afterward, Martin Luther King Jr. was killed, and I became fearful that my father might face the same fate. He worked full-time as a chauffeur and property caretaker for a wealthy white family with a house in the suburbs and an apartment in New York City. Throughout my childhood, he also continued his ministry work, starting as an assistant minister and eventually being assigned to his churches at various locations across the state.

They were storefront churches located in the inner city, often in areas that weren't always safe. I remember several times when they were vandalized and broken into, but this never deterred my dad. He was there to minister to the community. Eventually, he was assigned to a church with an established structure in a small community by the water, where he faithfully served for 18 years. Unfortunately, Alzheimer's, as we know it today, began to affect his mind, leading to his retirement. He was also diagnosed with early-stage prostate cancer, which was managed with medication. As Alzheimer's progressed, he could no longer suppress the emotions he had held onto for years, especially the deep pain of not knowing his mother, whose life ended as he began. He passed away just two weeks before my daughter was born, making way for her arrival into this world.

My father was a significant inspiration in my life. His example drove many of the things I've accomplished. I remember that during my last semester of college, I wanted to come home and finish school there. My mother was against the idea, but my father said, 'Nancy, just remember, it won't be as long as it has been. If you've come this far, you can surely make it to the end.' I've often recalled this advice when I've wanted to give up.

But I've also learned that inspiration must come from within. Often, it arises during **quiet moments of reflection, prayer, or meditation**. These moments provide me with clarity, and that clarity strengthens my voice.

Inspiration connects your voice to your purpose. Without it, your words may feel empty or lack direction. Inspiration fills your voice with **energy, creativity, and meaning.**

One of the most important things I've learned about inspiration is how it helps me overcome fear. Using your voice can be intimidating, especially in uncertain or uncomfortable situations. But when I'm inspired, I feel a deep sense of courage that drives me to speak up, even when it's complicated.

Inspiration connects us to something greater than ourselves. When I realize that my voice has a purpose beyond my fears or doubts, I feel empowered to use it. Inspiration helps me rise above fear and recognize that my voice has the potential to make a difference. It's not about avoiding fear but using inspiration to push through it.

***Isaiah 40:31** – "But those who hope in the Lord will renew their strength. They will soar on wings like eagles; they will run and not grow weary; they will walk and not faint."*

This is my favorite scripture, as it reminds me that when I am connected to God, He renews my strength. My voice becomes more than words—it becomes a tool for sharing hope, truth, and love with the world.

Inspiration is deeply connected to creativity. When I feel inspired, ideas flow more freely, and I discover new ways to express myself. This creativity enables me to communicate in unique and impactful ways. Whether through writing, speaking, or other creative activities, inspiration opens the door to endless possibilities.

I've learned that creativity is a powerful tool for self-expression. When you are inspired, new ideas seem to come effortlessly. This is why nurturing your creative side is so important—it allows you to elevate your voice in ways you never thought possible.

Inspiration can come from God, nature, relationships, or life experiences. I've discovered that my voice is most potent when deeply connected to the sources that resonate most with me. For example, spending time in church allows me to reflect on God's creativity, which, in turn, inspires me to be creative with my voice.

I've also realized that prayer and meditation are essential for keeping my inspiration flowing. When I take time to pray, I open myself to divine wisdom and guidance. This brings me clarity and motivates me to speak up when necessary.

Psalm 46:10 – "Be still and know that I am God."

In moments of stillness, I am reminded that God is my ultimate source of inspiration. During quiet times of reflection and prayer, I find the strength to use my voice with purpose.

One challenge I have faced is maintaining that sense of inspiration. Some days, it comes easily, while the spark feels absent on others. I've learned that staying inspired is not about waiting for the perfect moment—it's about actively seeking and nurturing sources of inspiration.

Whether reading scripture, spending time with inspiring people, or reflecting on past victories, staying connected to inspiration is critical to keeping my voice strong and clear. When I consistently inspire my spirit, I can use my voice more effectively, no matter the circumstances.

The most important lesson about inspiration is that it leads to action. It's not just about feeling inspired—it's about allowing that inspiration to move you to speak, create, and make a difference. Inspiration is the driving force that transforms thoughts into reality, and without action, it goes to waste.

James 1:22 – "Do not merely listen to the word, and so deceive yourselves. Do what it says."

This verse reminds me that inspiration should always lead to action. It's not enough to be inspired—I must use that inspiration to speak up, act, and fulfill my purpose.

When you speak from a place of inspiration, your words carry more weight. People can sense the authenticity, passion, and purpose behind your message. An inspired voice doesn't just communicate information—it moves hearts, challenges minds, and stirs souls.

I've learned that when I am inspired, my voice can become a catalyst for change. Whether I'm encouraging someone, standing up for what's right, or sharing my faith, an inspired voice can make a lasting impact.

Inspiration is not just a feeling—it's a divine spark that connects us to our purpose. When we tap into that inspiration, our voice transforms into a powerful tool for change, creativity, and influence. As you continue on your journey of using your voice, remember that inspiration is always within reach. Trust in God, your source of inspiration, to provide the guidance you need, and let that inspiration direct your words and actions.

Lessons Learned

- When I experience higher amounts of inspiration, I tend to have more compelling goals and make more progress in realizing them. It's another reason to keep challenging myself.
- Inspiration transforms my to-do list from things I have to do into things I want to do. My life feels more purposeful.
- Inspiration wakes me up to the beauty of daily life.
- Build my self-esteem. I have found that a healthy self-image is essential for inspiration. I accept and appreciate myself for who I am.
- I look on the bright side and focus on the things I can control.

- Being thankful is especially powerful. I keep a journal to remind myself of my blessings and let others know they make a difference in my life.
- Observe role models. Enthusiasm is contagious. I surround myself with friends and colleagues who are passionate about their work.
- I devote myself to lifelong education, reading books, and listening to podcasts about various subjects. I keep adding to my knowledge and skills.
- Try new things. Exploring unfamiliar territory helps me overcome fears and think more flexibly. I might substitute an exercise class for my usual walk or volunteer at a local food bank or animal shelter.
- Practice patience. Dramatic flashes and profound insights can be few and far between. I remember that gradual developments can also pave the way to success.
- Take action. On the other hand, I may sometimes speed up the process by taking a first step while waiting for inspiration to strike
- Limit competition. While there are many sources of inspiration, comparing myself to

others may backfire. I focus on enjoying my work and learning from my experiences instead of worrying about impressing others.

- I open up more possibilities because being inspired helps me accomplish great things and have more fun.
- I seek to be inspired each day. I am blessed to have this day and do everything possible to make the most of it. Learning more, creating projects and ideas, and being successful in my work are consistently on my mind.
- Rather than just sitting on the sidelines and watching my life go by, I jump into the thick of it and make things happen.
- I discover inspiration from many sources. I am open to knowledge on being a more effective parent, enlightened friend, and productive worker.
- I keep my mind open to new information. It's exciting to discover new knowledge about the subjects I'm interested in. To be inspired is to begin anew, working on those topics that light my creative fires.

- Today, my life is enriched because I seek inspiration daily. The newness I discover in my everyday life never ceases to amaze me.

Using *Your* Voice....

Inspiration fuels us when we feel weak, weary, or uncertain. It came through my father's legacy, nature, and the relationships around me. Staying connected to sources of inspiration—primarily through scripture—helped keep my voice strong and clear. Inspiration leads to action. When we allow ourselves to be inspired, our voices can move mountains, reminding us that we are part of something bigger than ourselves.

Reflection Questions:

- What sources of inspiration fuel your voice?
- How can you consistently nurture that inspiration?
- What action can you take today that is inspired by your calling?

Exercise: Nurturing Inspiration

Step 1: Identify Sources of Inspiration

Write down three things, people, or places that inspire you the most (e.g., scripture, nature, mentors).

Step 2: Create a Routine

List two ways you can consistently nurture your inspiration each week. This can include setting aside time for prayer, reading, or walking in nature.

Step 3: Inspired Action

Write down one action you can take this week that is fueled by your inspiration. This could be encouraging someone else, sharing your story, or starting a project that aligns with your calling.

CHAPTER SIX: COMMITMENT

Proverbs 16:3: "Commit to the Lord whatever I do, and He will establish my plans."

The high I experienced while transitioning from high school to college lasted about a week. For a while, everything felt perfect. My best friend from K-12 was there with me, and we were supposed to tackle this new chapter together. But a week later, she returned home to be with her boyfriend, whom she had started dating in her junior year. It felt like a betrayal, even though it wasn't. I was devastated, and without her, I withdrew completely. I would attend class, return to my dorm room, and isolate myself from everyone around me.

The small Black community at school knew each other and socialized together—except for me. I didn't make any effort to join in, so I earned a reputation. People started calling me **"stuck-up,"** I heard the whispers and felt the taunts as I walked to and from class. I just wanted to disappear, and I think I did in some ways.

Then, one of the girls from my dorm decided she wouldn't let me stay hidden. She and her friends began knocking on my door every evening, encouraging me to join them for dinner. Most of the time, I didn't eat much, but I went with them to avoid their persistent knocks.

One evening, she invited me to the library after dinner to study with her and a classmate. I didn't want to go, but she was relentless, so I agreed. She introduced me to her classmate, a guy I had never seen on campus. I quickly excused myself to study alone. Later, as the library was closing, this classmate approached me and asked if we could talk briefly. I hesitated but eventually agreed.

He told me he had heard the rumors about me being stuck up, but instead of believing them, he wanted to hear my story. He asked why I didn't socialize with anyone. I gave him a short version: my best friend had left, and I just wanted to be alone. He nodded with understanding and began sharing his own story. He explained that he only stayed on campus during the week for classes but traveled home every weekend to care for his great-grandparents, who had raised him. His great-grandfather was in his nineties, and his great-grandmother was in her eighties. His story was unimaginable to me.

As we continued to talk, I found myself intrigued by his values and the depth of his character. He was unlike any other young man on campus. We became fast friends, bonding over music and off-campus dinners. As our friendship grew, so did my feelings for him. It wasn't long before I distinctly heard God's voice telling me that this was the man I would marry. I kept that revelation to myself, believing that if it were true, he would eventually pursue me.

When I went home for Thanksgiving, I mentioned him to my parents—not as a boyfriend but as a good friend. My mother was ecstatic, convinced I was on the path to fulfilling her vision for me (remember the chapter on Vision). Upon returning to school, I told him I had mentioned him to my parents, and he asked what I had said. His reaction confirmed that he didn't share the same feelings for me.

I stayed committed to our friendship, even as he began dating other girls. It was painful, but I held on to the belief that if God had told me we were meant to be, it would happen in time. Shortly after Christmas break, his great-grandfather passed away. Four of us from school attended the funeral. It was the first funeral I had ever experienced, and seeing him collapse in grief broke me.

Weeks passed, and he eventually returned to campus. Our friendship continued, but he was clearly moving in a different direction. He started dating girls off-campus while I remained his constant friend. I began to question whether I had heard God correctly. How could this be the man I was supposed to marry if he wasn't pursuing me?

One day, he invited me to his home to meet his great-grandmother. When I stepped into their house, my heart skipped a beat. His great-grandmother looked exactly like my mother—an older version of her, but the resemblance was uncanny. She even had the same professional portrait my mother had taken, sitting in the same pose, framed on a side table. I felt as though I were looking at her twin. It felt like another sign from God that we were meant to be.

But despite all of this, he continued to date other women, and I remained in the role of his friend. He eventually left school to care for his great-grandmother full-time as her health started to deteriorate. I transferred to another school to complete my senior year, but our friendship remained strong.

Even after college, we stayed connected. My job required me to travel, and I would always find ways to stop in Cleveland, OH, where he had moved to be closer to family. I eventually met most of his family living there, including his girlfriends and eventually the one who would become his fiancée. He became a father to two children, and I stayed committed to being his friend, even though my heart was heavy with unspoken feelings.

Life moved forward for me as well. I became pregnant and married my children's father a year after he married his fiancée. He and I remained each other's confidant, sharing our struggles and victories. When his marriage eventually ended in divorce, I continued to support him from afar. Meanwhile, my marriage was struggling as my husband battled addiction, and we eventually separated.

I was committed to him, my family, and myself throughout this. I stayed connected to the man I believed God had told me would be my husband, even as life led us in different directions. Eventually, I expressed my feelings to him, and we began to discuss marriage, even though I was technically still married. I moved forward with my divorce and waited until my daughter graduated from high school to remarry.

Some might think I should have been committed to an institution at some point, given this saga. But through it all, God taught me about commitment. It wasn't just about romantic love; it was about agape love—the highest form of love and act of will. He carried deep wounds of abandonment, trauma, and mistrust; my commitment was to be a constant in his life, to show him the love of God through my actions, which he acknowledged and thanked me in the final days before he took his last breath.

Commitment isn't just about staying the course; it's about choosing to love, support, and be present for others, even when challenging. When using your voice, commitment keeps you speaking, believing, and showing up, no matter the obstacles. Without commitment, vision fades, opportunities slip away, and the strength to use your voice weakens. But with commitment, you find the power to persevere, to keep speaking, and to keep loving. It's what transforms our dreams, ideas, and passions into reality.

Lessons Learned

- I have learned that commitment is more than just a decision; it is an ongoing process. My daily choice is to show up, speak up, and stay true to God's voice.
- Commitment is a promise we make to ourselves and God. It is the decision to remain dedicated to a cause, goal, purpose, or person, regardless of the challenges that arise.
- Commitment keeps me anchored, even when I feel like giving up. It's what pushes me, even when I'm afraid or uncertain. Commitment is the driving force that ensures I follow through on purpose when using my voice.
- **Proverbs 16:3 – *"Commit to the Lord whatever you do, and he will establish your plans."***
- This scripture reminds me that when I commit my actions and voice to God, He will guide my steps. It's not enough to have a vision or a desire to speak; I must commit to it fully, trusting that

God will provide the strength and wisdom I need to see it through.
- Using my voice effectively requires consistency. It's not about speaking up once or twice and retreating into silence. It's about showing up daily, even when uncomfortable or inconvenient.
- I've realized that consistency is critical to building confidence in my voice and developing the courage to use it in all situations.
- **Galatians 6:9 – *"Let us not become weary in doing good, for at the proper time we will reap a harvest if we do not give up."***
- This verse reminds me that if I consistently use my voice for good, I will eventually see the fruits of my labor. Commitment means continuing to speak, even when no one is listening or progress is slow. God promises that my efforts will not be in vain.
- Fear is one of the biggest obstacles to using my voice. I have often hesitated to speak because I fear rejection, criticism, or failure. But commitment is what helps me push through that fear. When I commit to using my voice, I

consciously decide to move forward, even when fear is present.

- **2 Timothy 1:7 –** *"For God has not given us a spirit of fear, but of power and of love and of a sound mind."*
- God has equipped me with everything I need to overcome fear. Commitment is about trusting in that truth and refusing to let fear silence me. When I remember that God has given me a spirit of power, I can speak boldly, knowing He is with me.
- There have been times when I wanted to give up. But commitment is what kept me going. Perseverance is essential to using my voice because the journey is not always easy. There will be setbacks, disappointments, and moments of doubt, but commitment helps me to keep pressing forward.
- **James 1:12 –** *"Blessed is the one who perseveres under trial because, having stood the test, that person will receive the crown of life that the Lord has promised to those who love him."*

- This scripture encourages me to persevere, even when the road is difficult. God sees my efforts and promises to reward those who remain steadfast. Commitment means refusing to give up, even when the journey is hard.
- One of the most effective ways I've strengthened my commitment to using my voice is by setting clear, actionable goals. Without a plan, it's easy to get discouraged or lose focus. But I am more likely to stay committed when I have specific goals, even when obstacles arise.
- **Habakkuk 2:2 – *"Then the Lord replied: 'Write down the revelation and make it plain on tablets so that a herald may run with it."*** This verse reminds me of the importance of having a clear vision. When I write down my goals and make them plain, I have a roadmap that keeps me on track. Commitment becomes easier when I know exactly what I'm working toward.
- Accountability has been a game-changer for me when it comes to commitment. I've learned that I am more likely to stay committed when I have people who hold me accountable. Whether it's a

trusted friend, a mentor, or a support group, having someone to check in with can make all the difference.

- **Proverbs 27:17 – *"As iron sharpens iron, so one person sharpens another."***
- Commitment is easier when others encourage and hold us to our word.
- Discipline is the backbone of commitment. I've learned that commitment is not about relying on motivation because motivation can be fleeting. Instead, it's about cultivating discipline through daily habits. When I establish daily practices that support my commitment to using my voice, I am more likely to follow through, even when I don't feel like it.
- **1 Corinthians 9:25 – *"Everyone who competes in the games goes into strict training. They do it to get a crown that will not last, but we do it to get a crown that will last forever."***
- This verse reminds me that discipline is essential to achieving my goals. Just as athletes train daily for a prize, I must cultivate discipline to succeed in using my voice. Commitment

means training myself through consistent habits that support my purpose.

- There have been moments when I felt like my efforts were in vain. But commitment also means trusting in God's timing. I've learned that God works behind the scenes even when I can't see the immediate results. He is faithful, and He honors our commitment.

- **Ecclesiastes 3:1 – *"There is a time for everything and a season for every activity under the heavens."***

- This scripture reminds me that God's timing is perfect. I trust He will bring forth the fruit in time when I commit. My job is to stay committed, even when the results are not immediate.

- Commitment is not a one-time decision; it is a lifelong journey. It requires perseverance, discipline, and trust in God's plan. But the rewards of staying committed are immeasurable. When I look back on my journey, I can see how God has used my commitment to shape, strengthen, and help me make a difference in the lives of others.

- I encourage you to stay the course. No matter what challenges arise or how many times you feel like giving up, remember that God is with you every step of the way. He has given you a voice for a reason, and He will provide everything you need to use it for His glory.
- **Hebrews 10:23 –** *"Let us hold unswervingly to the hope we profess, for he who promised is faithful."*
- God is faithful to His promises, and when we commit our voice to Him, He will guide us toward fulfilling His purpose. Stay committed, stay faithful, and let your voice shine.

Use Your Voice....

Commitment is the glue that keeps your voice strong, even when challenges arise. Without commitment, vision fades, and opportunities slip away. God honors our commitment. When we dedicate our plans to Him, He will establish them. Using your voice requires not just passion but also persistence and discipline.

Reflection Questions:

- What areas in your life require greater commitment?
- How has commitment (or lack of it) impacted your ability to use your voice?
- What habits can you implement to strengthen your commitment to speaking up?

Exercise: Strengthening Commitment

Step 1: Assess Your Commitment

Write down two areas of your life where your commitment has wavered.

Step 2: Create a Commitment Plan

For each area, write one habit or practice you will implement to strengthen your commitment (e.g., journaling daily, setting a consistent time to speak or share your voice, practicing gratitude).

Step 3: Accountability Partner

Write down the name of one person who can help hold you accountable to your commitment. Reach out to them and share your plan.

CHAPTER SEVEN: ELEVATION

James 4:10 - "Humble yourself before the Lord, and He will lift you up."

ELEVATION – AMPLIFYING YOUR VOICE FOR GREATER IMPACT

Believe it or not, my banking career started with a fear of trying something I had never done before. My husband and I had just moved in with my parents to help my mom care for my father, who had Alzheimer's. Our local community bank, where I had my first savings account, was expanding and moving its headquarters to a brand-new facility. They were hiring tellers who would train at the current headquarters and later transfer to the new building once it was completed. Math had always been my Achilles' heel in school. I excelled in English and other subjects, but math was my weakest area. Despite that, I decided to give it a shot and start as a teller to see where it would take me.

That was 35 years ago. At the time, training involved standing next to a more experienced employee at the teller line, observing for a couple of weeks. Then, I was given my drawer beside hers while she watched me.

I observed her for a week before asking if I could start handling transactions using her cash drawer while she supervised. I did that for another week, and by the third week, she told me I was ready to have my drawer and work independently. I found the process relatively easy, and I enjoyed interacting with customers. As they continued to hire more tellers, I became a trainer in my fourth week, guiding new hires at the teller window while they watched me. By the sixth week, I was assigned to sit with employees at the sit-down desks to observe them opening new accounts. I shadowed them for a week as they opened new accounts.

The following week, they sat me in a conference room to watch videos covering the basics of compliance and banking laws. During this time, I found out I was expecting my second child. Management wasn't particularly thrilled with the news, as it meant I would be taking maternity leave at a critical time. However, for obvious reasons, they couldn't say much about it. By my 8th week in banking, I was opening new accounts and training other new hires to do the same. I enjoyed the challenge of learning something new. The head of retail banking, the only woman in a senior leadership position, observed me and guided my growth within the organization. She would become my mentor—and an excellent one at that.

Once we moved into the new building, she sat me down for my 90-day review. She expressed how impressed she was with my progress in such a short period and acknowledged my potential to achieve even more. I shared with her my need to increase my income to support my family better. She asked for some time, assuring me that more opportunities would arise as the organization grew. She also made it clear that she would advocate for me to reach my goals. And she did—masterfully.

Shortly after, she created a trainer position for retail banking, and I was assigned to develop and deliver all the training programs for tellers and new account representatives. She gave me the opportunity to take "train the trainer" courses, allowing me to further enhance my skills in this area. In addition, I took various banking courses to expand my knowledge of the industry. I participated in state banking schools at the time, which furthered my education. I also had the chance to hone my training and teaching skills by teaching for the American Institute of Banking.

As time passed, she realized that having tellers pause to assist customers in person while also handling phone inquiries wasn't providing the best service. She came up with the idea of starting a call center with dedicated staff to handle phone inquiries, offering a better solution. She approached me with the opportunity to implement the call center from the ground up. Her timing was always impeccable; I never had to express my need for a change—she could always sense it from my actions. While implementing the call center, I continued to serve as the trainer, but eventually, I had to make a choice. I decided to move forward with the call center.

The opportunity to hire, train, and develop people excited me. Soon, a new challenge arose: integrating our electronic banking operation into the call center. I embraced this challenge with enthusiasm and optimism, as in all previous opportunities. Eventually, the time came when I would no longer report to my mentor. It was difficult for her, as she had witnessed and taken responsibility for my growth and development as a professional. I reassured her that she had prepared me to take full responsibility for advancing my career with confidence, and I remain eternally grateful.

I then relocated to join my second husband, and soon after, I had the chance to work for a similar bank, managing a call center and onboarding electronic banking products and services. Once again, opportunities to advance presented themselves as I continued to work hard. It wasn't long before I was promoted to Assistant Vice President, Vice President, and ultimately, Senior Vice President.

For me, elevation wasn't about using my voice but working hard and being rewarded. This formula led me to every position I've achieved. But here's the turning point—I didn't believe I was worthy. As Jamie Kern Lima says in her book *Worthy*, ***"We rise to the level of our self-worth."*** This internal belief serves as our foundation, distinct from rising to the level of self-confidence, which is built on external factors. I mentioned this earlier in the Mindset chapter. This revelation has been the barrier behind my hidden fears, holding me back from moving forward with my purpose.

James 4:10 – "Humble yourselves before the Lord, and He will lift you up."

When we humble ourselves and commit our voice to Him, He gives us an internal foundation of self-worth and elevates us to fulfill His purpose.

I've come to realize that there are levels to expressing oneself, and as you grow, your voice must grow with you. Elevation involves refining, expanding, and using not only your actions but also your voice—not just for your benefit but for the benefit of those around you.

Elevation isn't reserved for public speakers, leaders, or influencers—it's for anyone who has something to say and the courage to say it.

Elevation is about amplifying the impact of your purpose through your voice. It's about rising above the obstacles, self-doubt, and limitations that once held you back and stepping into a more powerful version of yourself. Elevation isn't just about speaking louder or being more visible; it's about speaking with greater intention, effectiveness, and purpose. It's about using your voice to influence change and inspire others to take action. It lifts us, giving us the platform, strength, and wisdom to use our voice in ways we never thought possible.

One of the first things I've learned about elevation is that it requires humility. To elevate your voice, you must first acknowledge where you are and what's holding you back. I had to confront the reality that there were areas where my voice needed growth—whether it was in my confidence, my ability to communicate clearly, or my willingness to speak in challenging situations. Humility allows us to recognize our weaknesses so that God can help us strengthen them.

1 Peter 5:6 – "Humble yourselves, therefore, under God's mighty hand, that He may lift you up in due time."

This scripture teaches that elevation comes when we are willing to submit ourselves to God's process. Elevating your voice doesn't happen overnight—it requires growth, patience, and perseverance. God will lift us in His timing, but we must be willing to do the work.

As I've grown in my ability to use my voice, I've noticed that God opens new doors of influence. Elevation is not just about personal growth; it's about expanding your reach and impact. When God elevates your voice, He places you in positions where your words can influence more people. Whether speaking in front of a larger audience, mentoring others, or using your voice to advocate for change, elevation increases your capacity to make a difference.

Matthew 5:14 – "You are the light of the world. A town built on a hill cannot be hidden."

This verse reminds me that God calls us to be a light in the world. Elevation means shining your light even brighter, allowing your voice to be heard in places where it can make a difference. When you let God elevate you, you're no longer hidden—you become a beacon of hope, truth, and inspiration for others.

Lessons Learned

- Elevation doesn't happen in one giant leap—it happens through consistent effort and persistence.
- I've learned that to elevate my voice, I must show up every day, even when it's hard. Whether it's writing, speaking, or having meaningful conversations, the key to elevation is consistency. The more I use my voice, the more confident I become and the more opportunities I find to elevate my message.
- **Galatians 6:9 – *"Let us not become weary in doing good, for at the proper time we will reap a harvest if we do not give up."***
- This verse has been a source of encouragement for me. It reminds me that even when the journey feels long, there is a reward for persistence. Elevation is about staying the course, using your voice even when no one is listening or progress seems slow. In due time, the fruits of your labor will show.
- One of the first steps to elevating your voice is having a clear message. When I wasn't sure what I stood for or what I wanted to say, my voice was

scattered, and my impact was minimal. But it became easier to elevate my voice with confidence and purpose when I took the time to define my message—to get clear on what I wanted to communicate and why.

- **Habakkuk 2:2 – *"Then the Lord replied: 'Write down the revelation and make it plain on tablets so that a herald may run with it."***
- This verse reminds me of the importance of clarity. When your message is clear, people can understand and run with it. Elevation requires that you know what you stand for and communicate it in a way others can grasp.
- Elevation is not something we achieve alone. I've learned that building relationships and connections is crucial to elevating my voice. When I surround myself with people who believe in my message and support my growth, I find more opportunities to use my voice. Elevation often happens through collaboration and community.
- **Proverbs 27:17 – *"As iron sharpens iron, so one person sharpens another."***

- This verse reminds me that we sharpen one another. Elevating your voice requires building relationships with people who will challenge and support you and help you grow. It's through these connections that new opportunities for elevation arise.
- Elevation requires preparation. I've learned that opportunities to use my voice can come at any moment, and the more prepared I am, the better I can seize those opportunities. Whether practicing public speaking, refining my writing, or staying informed about the topics I care about, preparation has been key to elevating my voice.
- **2 Timothy 2:15** – *"Do your best to present yourself to God as one approved, a worker who does not need to be ashamed and who correctly handles the word of truth."*
- This scripture reminds me that preparation is essential to using my voice effectively. When I'm prepared, I can speak with confidence and authority, knowing that I have done the work necessary to elevate my message.

- One of the most important lessons I've learned about elevation is that it often comes through challenges. There have been times when I faced criticism, rejection, or uncertainty, but those moments of struggle were also moments of growth. Elevation requires embracing challenges as opportunities to refine and strengthen our voice.
- **Romans 5:3-4 – *"Not only so, but we also glory in our sufferings, because we know that suffering produces perseverance; perseverance produces character; and character produces hope."***
- This scripture reminds me that challenges are part of the process. It's through adversity that we grow, and it's through growth that we elevate. The more I embrace challenges, the more refined and impactful my voice becomes.
- The true elevation of your voice comes not when you use it for yourself but when you use it to help others. I've learned that the more I focus on advocating for, uplifting, and supporting those around me, the more impactful my voice

becomes. Elevation is about amplifying your voice for the benefit of others.

- **Philippians 2:3-4 – *"Do nothing out of selfish ambition or vain conceit. Rather, in humility, value others above yourselves, not looking to your own interests but each of you to the interests of the others."***
- This verse reminds me that elevation is not about self-promotion but service. God elevates me in return when I use my voice to elevate others.
- Elevation is not a one-time event; it's a continuous journey. As I've learned to use my voice, I've realized that elevation happens in stages. Each time I overcome a fear, seize an opportunity, or grow my understanding, I rise to a new level. God always calls us higher and wants us to use our voice to make a greater impact.
- As you continue on your journey of using your voice, remember that elevation requires humility, persistence, and a willingness to grow. Trust that God is with you every step of the way,

and He will lift you up as you commit to using your voice for His purpose.

- **Isaiah 40:31 –** *"But those who hope in the Lord will renew their strength. They will soar on wings like eagles; they will run and not grow weary; they will walk and not faint."*
- Let this scripture remind you that as you trust God, He will elevate you. Your voice, strengthened by His power, has the potential to soar to new heights and impact the world around you. Keep pressing forward, keep speaking, and keep rising higher.

Using Your Voice......

Elevation is about growing into the fullest expression of your voice. Every new opportunity, challenge, and step forward allows you to elevate your voice beyond where it was before. Elevation is also about service—using your voice not only for yourself but for the benefit of others. God will elevate us when we humble ourselves and stay committed to His purpose. Elevating your voice requires time, persistence, and trust in His timing.

Reflection Questions:

- How do you want to elevate your voice in the next season of your life?
- What are you doing today to prepare for that elevation?
- How can you use your voice to help others rise?

Exercise: Elevating Your Voice

Step 1: Define Elevation

Write down what "elevating your voice" means to you. How do you want your voice to make a more significant impact?

Step 2: Prepare for Elevation

List three steps you can take this month to prepare for the next level of using your voice (e.g., taking a public speaking course, mentoring someone, volunteering).

Step 3: Serve Others

Write down one way you can use your voice to uplift or support someone else this week. Commit to taking that action within the next seven days.

THE FINAL CHAPTER

THE POWER OF YOUR VOICE – A JOURNEY OF TRANSFORMATION

As I sit down to reflect on the journey of writing *You Have Something to Say... Use Your Voice*, I can't help but feel a deep sense of gratitude for all the experiences, lessons, and people who have shaped my life and given me the courage to use my voice finally. This book is more than just words on paper; it is a testament to the power of our voices and the unique roles they play in our lives. I've shared insights and deeply personal stories of struggle, triumph, and growth through each chapter. As we reach this final chapter, I want to weave together the threads of those lessons and stories to remind you of one important truth: You have something to say, and the world is waiting to hear it.

MINDSET: THE FOUNDATION FOR USING YOUR VOICE

Everything begins with a mindset. It's the foundation on which our lives are built, determining how we approach every opportunity, challenge, and interaction. For the longest time, I didn't realize that my mindset was keeping me silent. I didn't believe what I had to say mattered, and that belief shaped my reality.

But the mindset is powerful. Everything changed as I shifted my thinking and recognized the value of my **worth and voice**. I no longer saw myself as insignificant or unworthy of speaking up. Instead, I embraced the idea that my voice was necessary and that by using it, I could change my own life but also impact the lives of others.

Insight: Your mindset is the key to unlocking your voice. It allows you to see challenges as opportunities and failures as lessons. With the mindset of believing you are **worthy,** you realize that your voice has power, and using it is essential to fulfilling your purpose.

FEAR: CONFRONTING THE SILENT ENEMY

Fear is the silent enemy that keeps many of us from speaking up. I've experienced that fear of rejection, failure, and judgment firsthand. It kept me from using my voice for far too long. However, this journey taught me that we must confront fear to grow.

In the chapter on fear, I shared the story of my struggle in college—how I isolated myself after my best friend left and allowed the whispers of others to define me. I was paralyzed by fear: fear of being seen, fear of standing out. But it was in facing that fear, through small acts of courage, that I began to reclaim my voice.

Insight: Fear is a natural part of life but doesn't have to control you. When you face your fears and take small steps forward, you realize that fear loses its power. Even when you're scared, speaking up is the first step toward overcoming fear.

VISION: SEEING BEYOND THE PRESENT

Having a vision for your life and your voice is critical. Without vision, it's easy to drift through life, never fully realizing your potential or the impact you can have. When I began to clarify my vision, I discovered how my voice could be used to inspire, uplift, and encourage others.

In the chapter on vision, I discussed the importance of clarifying what you want to say and why it matters. Your vision is your guiding light, which keeps you moving forward when doubt creeps in. My vision has always been tied to helping others find their voice. I knew that if I could share my story, it would inspire others to share theirs.

Insight: Vision provides direction and purpose. When you clearly understand how your voice can impact the world, it gives you the strength to persevere, even when the path isn't easy. Take the time to define your vision—it will shape how you use your voice.

OPPORTUNITY: SAYING YES TO THE MOMENT

Opportunity often comes when we least expect it, and the key to using your voice is being ready to say ***"yes"*** when the moment arrives. After my husband passed away, I found myself at a crossroads. I had to choose: Would I retreat into silence or step into the opportunities presenting themselves?

In the chapter on opportunity, I shared how saying ***"yes"*** to joining a church, becoming a reinvention strategist, organizing my estate affairs, joining a women's spiritual support group, and writing this book all opened doors for me to use my voice in ways I never imagined. Each opportunity allowed me to speak up, share my story, and inspire others.

Insight: Opportunities to use your voice are everywhere, but you must be willing to say ***"yes."*** Even when it's uncomfortable and you don't feel ready, saying ***"yes"*** to opportunities allows your voice to grow and reach new heights.

INSPIRATION: THE FUEL FOR YOUR VOICE

Inspiration is the fuel that keeps us going, especially when the road gets tough. Throughout my life, I've found inspiration in unexpected places—through prayer, nature, scripture, and the people around me. These moments of inspiration have reignited my passion for using my voice.

In the chapter on inspiration, I discussed how staying connected to the sources of inspiration in your life is critical for keeping your voice alive. Through quiet moments of reflection, time spent with loved ones, or diving into the Word of God, inspiration helps us align with our purpose.

Insight: Inspiration is all around you, but you must be open to it. Stay connected to the things that inspire you, and let that inspiration fuel your voice. When you speak from a place of inspiration, your words can move mountains.

COMMITMENT: THE SILENT FORCE BEHIND YOUR VOICE

Using your voice requires commitment. It's not enough to speak up once and then retreat into silence. To make a lasting impact, you must remain dedicated to using your voice, even when it's complicated.

In the chapter on commitment, I shared the story of my long-standing relationship with my husband, despite life's twists and turns, remained a constant presence in my life. It taught me that genuine commitment isn't always easy but necessary. Commitment is what keeps you showing up, keeps you speaking, and propels you forward.

Commitment is the glue that holds everything together. Without it, inspiration fades, vision loses clarity, and opportunities slip away.

ELEVATION: RISING TO NEW HEIGHTS WITH YOUR VOICE

Elevation is about taking your voice to the next level. It's not just about speaking but amplifying your message and deepening its impact. Throughout this journey, I've learned that my voice must grow with me as I grow. Elevation involves refining, expanding, and using your voice not only for your benefit but also for the benefit of those around you.

In the chapter on elevation, I shared how God has elevated my voice in ways I never expected. Through humility, persistence, and preparation, I've risen above challenges and used my voice to inspire others. Elevation is about speaking with purpose and intentionality, knowing that God will lift you higher as you commit to using your voice for His glory.

Insight: Elevation requires growth, humility, and persistence. Trust that God will elevate you to new heights as you continue to use your voice. Your voice has the power to inspire, influence, and create change, but you must be willing to rise to the occasion.

YOUR VOICE MATTERS

As I come to the end of this book, I want to leave you with one final thought: ***You are worthy, and your voice matters***. It doesn't matter where you've come from, what you've been through, or how insignificant you may feel—your voice has the power to change lives.

Whether you're speaking up for yourself, advocating for others, or sharing your story, you are worthy, and your voice has the potential to make a difference. Don't let fear, doubt, or uncertainty hold you back any longer. Step into the opportunities that come your way stay committed to using your voice and trust that God will elevate you to new heights.

Use Your Voice....

1. **Take a moment to reflect on your own journey.**
2. **Where have you been holding back?**
3. **What opportunities have you said no to because of fear or doubt?**

Now, make a decision to say Yes!

- **Yes, to using your voice!**
- **Yes. to stepping into your purpose!**
- **Yes, to the impact you are meant to have in this world!**
- **You have something to say, and the world is waiting to hear it!**

Made in the USA
Monee, IL
28 February 2025